The Russian Alphabet Book

THE RUSSIAN ALPHABET BOOK

by Dr. Fan Parker

Illustrated by Nicolai Cikovsky

COWARD-McCANN, INC.   NEW YORK

The Russian Alphabet Book

How to say The Russian Alphabet

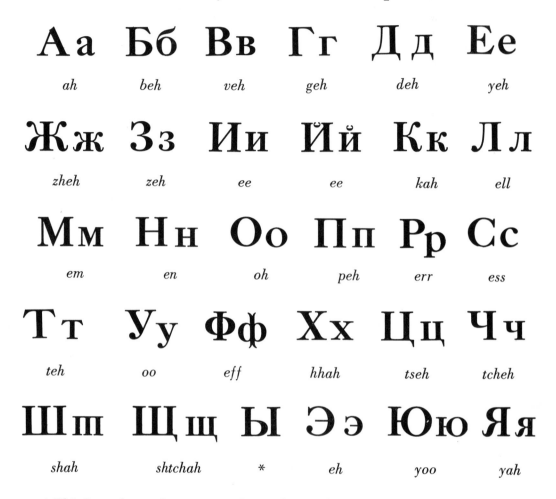

А а	**Б б**	**В в**	**Г г**	**Д д**	**Е е**
ah	*beh*	*veh*	*geh*	*deh*	*yeh*
Ж ж	**З з**	**И и**	**Й й**	**К к**	**Л л**
zheh	*zeh*	*ee*	*ee*	*kah*	*ell*
М м	**Н н**	**О о**	**П п**	**Р р**	**С с**
em	*en*	*oh*	*peh*	*err*	*ess*
Т т	**У у**	**Ф ф**	**Х х**	**Ц ц**	**Ч ч**
teh	*oo*	*eff*	*hhah*	*tseh*	*tcheh*
Ш ш	**Щ щ**	**Ы**	**Э э**	**Ю ю**	**Я я**
shah	*shtchah*	*	*eh*	*yoo*	*yah*

* This letter has a deep ee sound, peculiar to Russian.

There are three additional letters in the Russian alphabet besides those listed on this page and illustrated in this book: ё (yo) pronounced as in *yore*, the seventh letter in the Russian alphabet, which is usually written without the two dots; **Ъ** -hard sign, the twenty-eighth letter, which separates a vowel from a consonant for purposes of pronunciation; and the **ь** -soft sign, the thirtieth letter, which makes the preceding consonant soft (an apostrophe may replace this letter in transliteration).

Alma-Ata

Alma-Ata is the capital city of
Kazakhstan, an Asian Soviet Republic.
Semi-Oriental people live in this
beautiful country of fertile plains and
rugged mountains.

Алма-Ата

al-ma-*a*-ta

Б

Баку

ba-koo

Baku

Baku is the main port and center of the Soviet Union's greatest oil-producing region. However, it is not an ocean port, but is located on the landlocked Caspian Sea. Baku is the capital of Azerbaijan, another Asian Soviet Republic. Ruins of ninth-century Arabian fortresses stand near twentieth-century research institutes and technical schools.

В

Volga

The Volga is the Mississippi River of Russia, and the largest river in Europe. It carries factory, farm and forest products throughout the country. In earlier times, the Volga boatmen pulled the heavy barges up and down the river.

Волга

vol-ga

Г

Горький

gor-ky

Gorky

Gorky, called Nizhnii Novgorod up to 1932, is an ancient town, founded over 700 years ago. Located at the intersection of the Oka and Volga Rivers, it became famous for large and colorful fairs. The city was renamed in honor of the famous Russian writer Maxim Gorky.

Don

Дон

don

The Don is a famous river in European Russia. Wheat and timber are transported along the Don, as well as coal from the Don Basin, the greatest coal-producing region in this area. A large number and variety of fish are taken from the river in the winter. This is important for the country because, like most rivers in Russia, the Don freezes in November and remains frozen until April.

E

Ереван

yer-e-van

Erevan

Erevan is the capital of Soviet Armenia. This territory is one of the smallest in the USSR, but it has one of the highest mountains, Mt. Ararat, where, according to the Bible, Noah's Ark rested after the flood. Armenia was almost entirely farmland before the 1917 revolution but is now known for copper mines, canning factories and other industries.

Zhiguli

Zhiguli is a small mountain range rising in the middle Volga region. Long ago a geological upheaval created these wooded mountains which caused the Volga River to detour instead of running a straight route. This beautiful area is very popular with tourists.

Жигули

zhi-goo-li

3

Zagorsk

Загорск

za-gorsk

Zagorsk, a town not far from Moscow, is both a toymaking center and a center of religious pilgrimage. Thousands of worshipers continuously come to the ancient monastery surrounded by massive walls. The graceful Bell Tower is the center of a group of ornate buildings representing the architectural heritage of many different centuries of Russian history.

И

Irkutsk

The beautiful old city of Irkutsk is located in Siberia at the junction of the Irkut and Angara Rivers. After the Russians entered Siberia, three hundred and eighty years ago, Irkutsk was the starting point for the overland trail to China. Later it became a center for political exiles. Now Irkutsk is the hub of science, industry and culture in the midst of the Siberian frontier.

Иркутск

er-*kootsk*

Й

Йошкар-Ола

yosh-*kar*-o-*la*

Ioshkar-Ola

Ioshkar-Ola, deep in the heart of European Russia, is the capital of the Mari Associated Soviet Socialist Republic. An ancient people, the Mari have acquired a written language only in the last forty years. Ioshkar-Ola in the Mari language means Red City. Today it is a center of the vitamin industry of the Soviet Union.

Kiev

К

Kiev is the capital of the Ukraine, but has been called the mother of Russian cities. Third in size, it stands first in historical significance. From Greece, the Russian Orthodox religion penetrated this vast country, and Kiev was the first metropolitan center where Christianity was established. Today the ancient citadel of Christianity, the Kiev-Pechersk Monastery, still stands.

Киев

ki-yev

Л

Leningrad

Ленинград

len-in-grad

Leningrad, originally called St. Petersburg, is one of the world's most beautiful cities. Founded by Czar Peter the Great in 1703, the city is built at the delta of the Neva River. Leningrad has 500 bridges and over 101 islands. Its location as both a sea and river port makes it one of the largest industrial as well as cultural centers in the Soviet Union.

M

Moscow

Moscow is the political, cultural and social center of the Soviet Union. It was named the capital after the 1917 revolution. Founded more than eight hundred years ago, the city was surrounded by the Kremlin walls in the same year that Columbus discovered America. Red Square was so named because the ancient Russian words for "red" and "beautiful" were the same. Moscow is also famous for its institutions, such as the Bolshoi Theater and ballet school, the Moscow Art Theater, the Moscow University, and the Academy of Sciences of the USSR.

Москва

mosk-*va*

H

Нева

nev-a

Neva

The Neva River is very important to the Soviet Union. Only 50 miles long, it is an outlet to the sea and navigable by large ocean liners. The Neva is also connected to inland waterways of the Soviet Union by numerous canals.

Odessa

Far from any ocean, Odessa is one of the major seaports and shipbuilding cities of the Soviet Union. It is situated on the Black Sea. Because of its temperate climate and pleasant beaches, Odessa draws about one hundred and fifty thousand vacationers annually. Some come for treatment at the mud baths.

Одесса

o-dess-a

23

П

Полтава

pol-*ta*-va

Poltava

Poltava is famous as the scene of the battle in which the armies of Peter the Great defeated Charles XII of Sweden in 1709. Poltava, in the Ukraine, is an important railway junction between Kiev, Kharkov Kremenchug and the Donets Basin. The city was primarily an agricultural crossroads before the revolution, but today has numerous industries. Nikolai Gogol, the famous Russian writer, received his early education in Poltava and many institutions are named after him.

24

Rostov

ros-tov

Rostov the Great is so called to distinguish it from the seaport city of Rostov-on-the-Don. It stands on the shore of Lake Nero about a hundred and twenty-five miles from Moscow. Originally settled by Finns and later colonized by Slavs, the city is well known for the market gardens of its suburbs which produce peas and chicory for export. The Rostov Kremlin or citadel is a fine example of Russian architecture.

C

Сталинград

stal-in-grad

Stalingrad

Stalingrad won its permanent place in world history when the Russians destroyed the Nazi forces there in 1942. The city was entirely rebuilt after the war, for almost every building had been destroyed in the battle. Situated on the Volga River, Stalingrad is now an important industrial city. The completion of the Volga Don Canal gave a fresh impetus to the city's growth and prosperity.

T

Tula

Tula is an ancient town about a hundred and twenty miles south of Moscow. Nearby is Yasnaya Polyana, the estate of Leo Tolstoy, now maintained as a national shrine. Tula gained recognition many years ago as the place where the best of the Russian samovars were manufactured. Today, in Tula, factories also produce rifles, pistols, ammunition and machine tools.

Тула

too-la

У

Уфа

oo-fa

Ufa

Ufa is the capital of the Bashkir Autonomous Soviet Socialist Republic, located on the eastern fringe of European Russia. The colorful Bashkir people are of Turkish origin and Moslem faith. For centuries they have almost lived in the saddle and they have the unusual ability to raise and use half-wild horses for military and other purposes.

Frunze

Frunze is the capital of the Kirghizia
Autonomous Soviet Socialist Republic,
which has a common frontier with
China. The mountainous region con-
tains some of the highest peaks in the
Soviet Union, including Mt. Stalin or
Tengri Khan, nearly 25,000 feet above
sea level. The Kirghiz are distinct people allied to the Mongols. Frunze has
a picturesque location on the slopes of
a mountain range and is the largest
industrial and cultural center of the
Republic.

Фрунзе

froon-ze

X

Харьков

khar-kov

Kharkov

Kharkov is one of several large cities in the Ukrainian Soviet Republic. Its university was established in 1805 and is one of the oldest in the area. The city is located near the Donets iron and coal region and has developed its industries and commerce rapidly. Kharkov is also a center of culture and learning in the Ukraine.

Tsei

Цей

tsei

Tsei is a health and vacation resort high in the mountains of the North Ossetin Autonomous Soviet Socialist Republic, in the south of European Russia. The Ossets, the people for whom the region is named, are of Persian ancestry and have their own language and cultural identity. The resort area is popular because of magnificent pine woods and unusually clear mountain air.

Ч

Chita

Чита

chi-*ta*

Chita, in Far Eastern Siberia, is the capital of the Independent Far Eastern Republic, which was annexed by the Soviet Union in 1922. Located on the Chita River, the city gained notoriety in the nineteenth century as the place where many political prisoners worked and died. Silver and gold mines were located and developed late in the nineteenth century, and Chita now has over 80 industrial enterprises.

Shadrinsk

Shadrinsk is just over the Ural Mts. in Siberia and fifteen miles away is the site of the Shadrinsk Experimental Station, headquarters of agricultural research and development for much of the Soviet Union. Scientists at this station have discovered and promoted new and improved methods of sowing and soil enrichment. They are supervising and conducting continuous experiments in nearby Soviet and collective farms in the constant search for increased productivity of the soil in the cold climate.

Шадринск

shad-rinsk

Щербаков

shcher-ba-*kov*

Shcherbakov

Shcherbakov, in the upper reaches of the Great Volga River, was known as Rybinsk until 1946. This region was so rich in fish that in the sixteenth century a village of freedmen was founded who were given the privilege of earning their livelihood as fishermen. The city is now a port and industrial center, specializing in the production of printing machines.

Ытык-Кель

Ytyk-Kel

Ытык-Кель

ytyk-kel

Ytyk-Kel is located in the Yakut ASSR near the capital of Yakutsk. This republic, more than one third the size of the United States, is the largest in Siberia and has the most severe climate. The good fishing along the rivers and on the coast combined with trapping, hunting and deer breeding provides support for the local population. Gold, platinum, diamonds and other minerals in this area make Siberia one of the richest lands in the Union.

Э

Электросталь

e-lek-tro-stal

Elektrostal

Elektrostal, a city in the vicinity of Moscow, was renamed because of its huge electrometallurgical plant, which manufactures high-quality steel. New blast furnaces were put into operation and modern equipment is available. Besides steel production the plant carries on scientific research in the attempt to forge and find practical application for new types of steel.

Ю

Yur

Yur, deep in Siberia, is a gold-mining town much like early mining communities in the western United States. It is located in the southeast portion of the Yakut ASSR, a region rich in various minerals. The climate is very severe and there is little agriculture.

Юр

yur

Я

Ялта

yal-ta

Yalta

Yalta is located on the Crimean peninsula in the Black Sea. It is sheltered by high mountains on the north and east, and has a record number of sunny days per year. Surrounded by palaces, parks, gardens and woods, Yalta is known as a "recuperating station" by the Soviet people. Roosevelt, Churchill and Stalin made history in Yalta in February 1945.

History

862	Beginning history of the ancient Russian state. A Viking prince, Rurik, was invited by the eastern Slavs to come to govern. With Rurik begins the first Russian dynasty.
988	Russians converted to Christianity in the eastern Byzantine form.
1237–1240	Mongolian conquest of Russia.
1240	Alexander Nevski defeats the Swedes on the Neva River.
1328	Moscow rises to prominence among Russian cities.
1480	Ivan III overthrows Mongolian domination.
1533–1584	Reign of Ivan IV, known as Ivan the Terrible. Crowned first Czar of Russia, 1547. A major achievement is conquest of Siberia.
1613–1645	Reign of Michael Romanov, grandnephew of Ivan the Terrible. Begins Romanov Dynasty which lasts until 1917. Serfdom firmly established.
1667	Revision of Russian liturgical books in accordance with original Greek sources. Those who oppose revision split from Mother Church.
1689–1725	Reign of Peter the Great, Czar of all Russia. St. Petersburg founded, 1703. Wins battle of Poltava, 1709. Obtains west shore of Caspian Sea, 1722.
1762–1796	Reign of Catherine II, Catherine the Great. Extends Russian territory to shores of Black Sea. Retakes all southwestern Russian lands.
1801–1825	Reign of Alexander I, who defeated Napoleon. Noted for liberal reforms.
1825–1855	Reign of Nicholas I.

1855–1881	Reign of Alexander II. Serfdom abolished 1861.
1881–1894	Reign of Alexander III. Most reactionary Russian period. Revolutionary organizations gain in strength.
1894–1917	Reign of Nicholas II, last Czar of Russia. Vladimir Lenin forms Bolshevik party, 1903. 1905, Russian revolution begins, but fails. 1917, Lenin seizes power. Russian Soviet Federative Socialist Republic formed.
1914–1918	World War I.
1918–1920	Civil War.
1921–1928	New economic policy. Trade with foreign nations.
1924	Lenin dies. Stalin emerges as leader of Communist party.
1928	Introduction of first Five Year Plan.
1934	Soviet Union enters League of Nations.
1936	Stalin constitution accepted.
1939	Soviet Union signs nonaggression pact with Germany.
1941	German Army attacks Soviet Union. Russia enters World War II.
1943	Stalin, Roosevelt, and Churchill meet at Teheran.
1945	End of World War II. Potsdam and Yalta conferences.
1953	Death of Stalin.
1955	Rise of Khrushchev to power.
1957	Soviet scientists place Sputnik in orbit.
1958	Khrushchev assumes Premiership.
1959	Khrushchev visits United States.
1960	Heads of Communist countries meet in Moscow.